"Agony and beauty are often two s
this searing collection of poetry K(
her struggles with anorexia nervos
cri de coeur and an inspirational beu...
the "macabre reality" of the illness."

Robert McMillen - The Irish News

"With poetry, prose and Biblical breadcrumbs of hope, Kathryn's words are somehow both delicate and hard hitting in the same breath. This is poetry - an author baring her soul on a page and inviting us to look in. Kathryn is a poetic tour guide, sharing her 'darkest valley' moments, yet with courage she clings on to the one true Comforter and invites us to do the same."

Dai Woolridge - Poet, Author and Storyteller

"Kathryn has created an extraordinary collection of poems here – extraordinary because the courage, honesty, humility, eloquence and beauty displayed in these pieces of writing are far from ordinary. I am so grateful to Kathryn for taking the time to weave together these captivating words, words which offer helpful insights to those who know little of this horrible mental illness and words which can offer encouragement and hope to those who share Kathryn's struggles. I sense that writing these poems has provided some restorative catharsis for Kathryn; I pray that this theme of hope-filled release will bring a measure of healing to readers who wrestle with this or similar mental illnesses."

Rev.d Will Souter - Vicar, Urban Crofters Church

"What a beautiful piece of work. It is brutally honest and although sometimes harrowing and very sad, still inspires hope and optimism. As a Peer Mentor Kathryn has helped, supported and inspired others at their darkest times. By publishing these poems and the account of her personal journey she will indeed help many more. Kathryn is such a positive role model not only those who have suffered with anorexia nervosa, but to all those who suffer with their own mental health demons in whatever form. Kathryn certainly is a strong person who we can all take lessons from."

Helena Lane - Growing Space, Mental Health Charity

It's Not Just Celery

By Kathryn Gonzales

From the Author

It's Not Just Celery is a collection of poems and personal extracts about me, Kathryn, negotiating life while simultaneously striving to keep Anorexia Nervosa in remission. This illness, which first presented in me as a teenager is, in actuality, nothing to do with food itself and yet is inextricably entwined with it, meaning in reality it is everything to do with food. It infiltrates every aspect of just trying to be. I now live on, seeking to celebrate each gloriously sacred day, despite this deadly disease lurking in the wings.

As my Grampa used to say, "forward we go."

It's Not Just Celery

It's Not Just Celery
Copyright © 2023 Kathryn Gonzales

All rights reserved.
No part of this book may be reproduced or used in any manner without the prior written permission of the copyright owner, except for the use of brief quotations in a book review.

To request permissions, contact the author via email at kljgauthor@gmail.com

Paperback ISBN: 9781803522579
First paperback edition: March 2023
Publisher: Independent Publishing Network
Publishing house: All Create Publishing
Cover and internal artwork: Rachel Rasmussen

Printed in the UK

Table of Contents

Introduction	9
Shadow	15
Placebo	25
Island	33
Checkmate	45
Liberation	61
And where to begin	73

Introduction

My paradoxical encounter since being on this planet. Anorexia Nervosa has been both my protector and poisoner for the majority of my precious days to date, decades have passed since I was a teen.

If these poems and personal extracts of mine even hint at unveiling the macabre reality of this illness and help to rekindle faith within those affected, be it directly or indirectly, that you are seen, you are heard, you are believed and peace and love are yours for the taking, then my purpose in this brief beautiful episode we call life has been fulfilled.

I have taken so many with me on this blur of silent inconsolable agony. The guilt rips through my soul, piercing the core of my being. It never stops, never lessens, never lets me forget. This illness is no one's fault and yet I blame myself. Perhaps I am a little crazy after all. I am extreme, intense, too much. I have lost many friends because of my erratic behaviour, explosive emotions and inability to coherently explain why I behaved so badly. I am learning everyday to find the words now. Sometimes, when those words come, I allow myself to speak. It is this catch-22 scenario that propels my implosion to greater heights and makes me default to my taciturn state. Balance remains an elusive concept to me. Note to self, pause, breathe, let it go.

For as long as I can remember, possibly from birth, I have existed here, in the milky way, in a permanent state of fear, utterly devoid of self-worth. I was blank. Feeling nothing, yet everything. A mind that never stops, but creates stagnancy. I was born on a Wednesday, the child full of woe. A disturbed joke, but morbidly apt. I am supposed to hate it, fight it. I did, I have, I do.

Every cell of me has been saturated with planning my snacks, organising my menu for every single meal, every single day. I have to assess everything. I now accept that I need to eat to honour the gift of life I have been given. Without my bespoke food preparation and examination process, I am unable to eat. My nerves spasm, electrified with sheer terror, paralysed in 'Nervosa.' Pain charges through my abdomen as if a vice is clamped around my stomach twisting tighter, tighter. Nausea ripples through my body, my head pounds in protest, a staccato rhythm creeps into my lungs. I inflict physical pain on myself through such infected thoughts. I create my own misery. I am my own enemy. I am my only chance for freedom. For me, going without is a breeze. Hunger has no bearing on me. It is so much easier for me than all this, trying to carry out what is for most a basic, yet fundamental human action and innate need. Trying to eat, allowing myself to be nourished. Hello God, our Father, I am sorry.

Managing this monster, and it is indeed a tyrant like no other, with years of lived experience having made its mark, is my most honest way of being able to live as me in the fullest way I know how. I rely on my 'simple, systematic, selection, strategy' to keep me out of the danger zone. The danger zone being where I foolishly allow even more precious presence to ebb away by attempting to deviate from this, daring to mix things up and finding myself for the trillionth occasion being physically and psychologically unable to do so. So, I go without instead. This bespoke survival strategy is my peace. Dysfunctional yes, irresponsible no. Without this, I would no longer be of this world.

Journalist Emma Woolf refers to Anorexia Nervosa as a 'young person's game' in her book 'An Apple a Day.' Whilst respecting Emma's opinion, I feel I am in a position to be able to say this is not a game. This is not a fun recreational hobby or diet fad. It is life and death. And this may help to begin to unravel why Anorexia Nervosa has historically been and still is to this day so difficult to treat, such is its complexity in manifestation and the fact that it carries one of the highest fatality rates of any other mental illness. Everyone is petrified of it. No one knows what to do. No one wants blood on their hands.

Anorexia Nervosa, I have come to understand, does not want me to engage with life, to embrace the blessing of being. Anorexia, in particular for me, rather demands I identify with the pivotal belief that I am essentially flawed, lacking in substance and consequently, at fault for the imperfections of our world. This breeds a vastness of vulnerability in me that smothers my senses in entirety. Denying myself life-sustaining needs, principally the need to eat and the need to drink, is the perfect antidote to exterminating this vulnerability and freezing out life. I go to battle daily, emerging quietly hour by hour to overcome these irrational, treacherous states, trying to craft connections with the living, gripping hold so they become entrenched in me. For every day that passes, I feel a winner, I am a winner. I continue to be eternally grateful that I am, that I remain. So many other unexpectant folk are not as fortunate. They are utterly consumed and devoured by the illness, as I have been, in mind body and spirit. They never make it home or see the light ever again. I pray for each and every one I of you. You are not forgotten.

Shadow

The child that never was

Never wants, never asks, never spoken,
It was me that was broken.
Shh, I can't hear you.

'Don't leave me please,' I beg,
I am the echo within my head.
Where is this place?

I must fit in, I must not stray,
I only know I'll lose my way.
Am I real? Am I here?

I must be good, I must agree,
I am nowhere, 'help' I plea.
Too late t'is done, I am adrift.

Inside my head, forever dread,
Roots blackened, seemingly dead.
Forgotten, detached, never known.

Not a season to be joyful

Christmas, the magnifying glass of self-sabotage.
Absent merriment,
Mathematical overload,
Meticulous mind mapping of every morsel,
Trust yourself, trust no one.
Calculus conundrums clog my senses,
Guilt grips my neck like a noose,
I cannot breathe.
When will this torturous nightmare cease?
Where is the joy?
I am an oddity. But I do not care. Not anymore.
That's a lie.

Barge pole

I am contaminated,
I am crawling with defection,

I am not deserving,
I am toxic,
I am unchartered territory,
I waste my chance of peace,
I am losing allies,
Fight or surrender.
My choice.

The destruction business

The curse of Anorexia Nervosa,
Obsessive, deceitful, relentless,
The master of manipulation,
Perfection in pretending,
Dismembering of any relationship held dear,
Casualties multiply around the infection,

It is never satisfied,
Self contempt festers,
The road to extinction ensues,
The cockroach triumphs.

Fear

Endless, heavy, suffocating,
I am drowning, everyday,

Again, again, again,
The cruelty of feeling cuts me,
Like the skewer, the blade, the tin,
Each is different and yet the same,
Etching me with my wretchedness,
I am vile, I am devastated,
I am a match in this world,
Intoxicating insomnia stamps on my spirit,
Sadness permeates my soul,
Are you listening now?

Psalm 34 : 18

The [Lord] is close to the broken-hearted
And saves those who are crushed in spirit

Placebo

To section or not to section, is that the question?

My legs no longer carry me,
My organs and muscles fuelling my very survival,
Powers behind the sanctity of life are smarter that I,

An emaciated doll,
Tracing paper skin, crumpled, sinewy,
A scalp decorated humbly with sparse wispy strands,
Teeth protruding through sallow grey hollows,
Spine crumbling, my humpback awaits,
A shrivelled corpse.

Conformed and still lost

Attend all medical appointments,

Check.

Participate in psychiatric treatment,

Check.
Be positive they say,
Such words drive mortality's edge closer,
Desperate to scream, yet my voice remains absent,

I am at war with myself,
Blackness swallows me whole,
Mummified in this quagmire.

Mercy

Just disappear,
Vanish, I hold no value,
A non-entity,
I have no essence,
I am empty,
Numbness is my only companion,
Chaos blinds me,
My fight feels futile,
Separating to survive,
Embodying awkward just to exist,
Bless every being who stopped to help,
You are angels of patience,
You are guardians of humility.

I'm sorry I scared you,
I'm sorry I drove you away.

Science and sponsors

The human brain, a maze of history,
Consciousness itself an elusive mystery.

Nature, our creative and our base,
Nurture, our cards, shuffle and place.

Money talks, lies told,
Deals struck, souls sold.

Narrative set, data collated,
Figures formed, picture painted.

Judgements build, then rated,
Lives taken and disintegrated.

Psalm 112 : 4

Even in darkness light dawns for the upright,
for the gracious and compassionate

Island

The gentle tornado

Shopping, oh shopping, an endurance event,
Prison cell pro-forma strobe my vision,
My eyes are wide, yet I cannot see,
The collision within me enters overdrive,
I am deafened and yet every sound shatters my core,
Six market visits over two days just for daily bread,

I select, I examine, I replace,
Repeat, repeat, repeat,
I blink to diffuse and disguise my torment,
It is exhausting, it is crippling,
I am humiliation,
Curator of disappointment,

I promise never to do it again,
Another promise broken.

The space in between

See,
Am I awake now?
Is this it?
Unravel this tapestry,
Slowly,

The dust forever coating my larynx,
Breathing still a forgettable chore,

Time is this,
Heal my oozing wound,
Expose my disfigurement,
Unlock these rusted chains.

Vagabond

Observing life from the outside in,
But frankly, really not doing that thing,
Living, breathing, getting in the frame,
Why is laughing for me so lame?
Spurring incoherent conversation,
The spotlight scolding me like annihilation,
The scaffolding of my silhouette,
Mirroring an overexposed fishing net,
Brittle, porous, overused,
Dripping in tenacity,
Revolting wholly suspect pity,
I know I incinerated my lowly last chance,
I am on my knees, begging for a pass,
Let me in I promise to be good,
I will look after myself and stop wearing my hood,

Gone is the uniform of passing hues,
I experiment in spectrum now: reds, yellows, blues,
Hosting a collage of breakage and branding,
My body is exhibit A, a blessing for comprehending.

Alone

I yearn to celebrate in sustenance,
To share in the indulgence of nourishment,
Ever the stranger to these blissful exchanges,
The raw spite of pain snapping at my heart,
I clutch to memories of such wonder as an infant,
I claw at the shame that smothers my way back,

Ostracised,
I am the alien,

I am erasing my being.

Psalm 34 : 5

Those who look to [Him] are radiant
Their faces are never covered with shame

Vulnerable and vacant

Love is a catalyst, love is select,
Love is the home I instinctively reject,
I am sorry my darling, my life, my one,

For letting you down, for becoming undone,
For all the excuses, the moments I shattered,
For doubting us, allowing us be battered,
Knowing your heart as I do,
I pray for your forgiveness to help us stay true.

Ricochet rainbow

Hypnotic beams flood my mind,
Halting time for me, how kind.

Shattering the insurmountable quo,
Conquered by courage I grow to know.

My zest for life hovers at terminal pace,
The comfort of gratitude cradles my face.

We are all energy forms individually made,
Every particle uniquely laid.

I hear my heart drumming so strong,
Outstretched with hunger for love to belong.

Over the decades, I have explored, experimented with, relied upon and adapted numerous psychological teachings, alternative therapeutic methods and even grown to embrace the love and kindness of others. However, such strands of support in isolation, I have found lose potency against Anorexia Nervosa, the trespasser that invaded my life as a child. I feel safe and confident to now share that my saving grace in empowering me with unyielding strength to face forward and continue learning to manage this illness has been opening my heart to have faith and lay trust in God. It has been the key to connecting the phases in my life, occupying the formally missing part of my heart that, until now, had been buried.

Checkmate

Agenda amnesty

Where did all the honesty go?
Transparency, trust, so much now a 'no',
Opinion and fact morphing into one,
Igniting assumption, emotion, all becoming undone,
Translation, perception, interpretation,
A glimpse at the elements in the equation,
Scripture, text, evidence built,
Still refuted in unconscious guilt,
Stuff, things, so many possessions,
Taking over, becoming obsessions,
Automated everything,
No substance, no zing,
Barefoot living provides our elation,
And the doorway to our salvation,
Honouring the aged, the wisdom that brings,
Seems to be wasted and thrown in the bins,
Momentum is bracing we know what is right,
Get ready for your awakening and living like a kite.

Simplicity is not simple

The epitome of irony in merely being,
A contradictory term intending to be freeing,
One step, one stride, continue toward the bend,
Follow the fragments, not the trend,
Beginning with the fullness of free will,
A starting block for the masses pending still,
Shortchanged of this apparent qualified right,

Abandoning our neighbours in their plight,
The choices in towers and behind artificial screens,
Dampening prospects, erasing dreams,
With the appetite for cyber to dominate all we know,
So, this faceless playground continues to grow,
Eroding tangible connections, mutating authentic source,
Normalising judgmental feuds, taking over by force,
A platform perpetuating mistrust to rise,
Endangering the fundamentals of faith to capsize,
Our essence, our creation will not be laid to rest,
By this misguided, disconnected illusion of our nest.

Proverbs 24 : 26

An honest answer is like a kiss on the lips

With all the devastation my eating disorder has caused to everything and everyone I hold dear, and all the years of distress I take responsibility for causing, giving space in my heart for God awards me with the gift I am in greatest need of. Forgiveness.

It's Not Just Celery

Wisdom

๑

I perch on the edge of insanity,
Waiting for the dawn of clarity,
The power of thought, the human mind,
A mesmerising driver often not kind,
To pause my brain and incessant thinking,
Is the greater force to stop me sinking,
So, thank you bullies for saving me,
I learned an abundant amount from thee,
You may not know who you are,
But I forgive you from afar,
I share this with you, not because you're bad,
But because I understand you were sad,
I pray for you as I do my own,
Ever hopeful for all to find the way home,
We are the same, you and I,

Human beings with souls that cry,
We are created and made of love,
Craving safety, warmth, the zen of a dove.

Perfection is...

Not an airbrushed image or adulterated face,
Nor a knitted cardie, no stitch out of place,
Neither is this word, this noun,
A dimension that even exists in town,
It cannot be attained through competitive drive,
To be better than your neighbour, feeding such pride,
This fictitious formula that leads to demise,
Creates only harm and even tells lies,
It cultivates a fragile way of surface-living,
The ultimate barrier to the joy of giving.

A sterile method of provision,

Generating sustained division,
Perfection in humanity is but a pretence,
Taker of tranquility and upholder of no sense,
Like leaving chocolates in the sunshine,
We are losing our minds, our way to the divine,
So, wriggle free of that starched strait jacket,
That mirage of status, importance and racket,
Instead lift your gaze, be in awe of that tree,
As this is where perfect will always be.

Brake please, hazard ahead

Signs, sounds, odours, gestures,
Words, silence, colours, textures,
All corridors of communication,
With power to transform our foundation,
This jigsaw puzzle of language tools,
Is our compass against meandering fools,
Bridge building can entrench our bliss,
Protect from harm, hurt, all that's amiss,
Time is that unstoppable force,
It dictates our world without remorse,
Waiting now is branded a sin,
Pop up lives, fast lane, what a din,
Consider this, that passerby is you,
Introduce yourself, take the cue,
We are all the gaps in between,
The links however seldom seen,
Rejoice in how our hearts sing on,
Carrying us as days go on,

There are no words that can encapsulate,
The phenomenal form we demonstrate,
To ignore this gift is a mournful affair,
We can change this together, we can repair.

It's Not Just Celery

Psalm 3 : 3

But you are the shield around me, O Lord, you bestow glory on me and lift my head up

It's Not Just Celery

Having navigated through a global pandemic, welcoming God's love into my life has been like stumbling upon the protected sanctuary of safety and belonging. I feel this acknowledgement is the most important reconciliation with life itself I have made, helping me to continue moving towards a lasting presence of peace and compassion.

Liberation

Life is every moment

Hello, my love, I have arrived,
It took this long because it lied,
To me, to you, to life and being,
Believing in nothing, estranged from all feeling,

But I am strong, you see this now,
A warrior before you with a puff of pow!
Learning from our world forever,
Evolving in peace, absorbing life together.

Faith

To focus forward is my cherished view,
To keep try, try, trying is my constant cue.

Love is the breath of life, its beauty,
Fighting my foe is my absolute duty.

Never relent to the abyss, never submit,
I choose the light, it is life to which I commit.

My husband

You are me, I am you,
You showed me love, it is true,
I cannot convey in words or ways,
The gratitude I feel all days,
Toward you my darling, my world, my life,
For loving me through all the strife,
My heart still beats because we are one,
You brought me life, you taught me fun,
Thank you, my love, for your very being,
You are my breath, my body, my all-new seeing.

It's Not Just Celery

Psalm 37 : 23 - 24

If The [Lord] delights in a man's way,
he makes his steps firm;
though he may stumble, he will not fall
For the Lord upholds him with his hand

Beyond this

🌿

Labels and identities,
Extra layering of entities,
Catapult our conflicted lands,
Into dangerous mercenary hands,
This propaganda poster of life direction,
Promising equity, justice and self-reflection,
Is not our handbook to know who we are,
Or interpret ourselves in the universe so far,

We are beyond these concepts of what life's about,
We are not caricatures created to shout,
So, listen for the pause and follow this sound,
Look for the space and allow it to ground,
We are the energy, the life force to unite,
The masterpiece of dazzling delight.

It's Not Just Celery

I am learning to trust and accept that whatever happens, God, our father, our intelligent designer, our creator, will always be there for me, transcendent with love. I may never be alone again. Without my faith, I know I would not be able to keep fathoming the strength to strike onward. But I know now I can, I will, I must. Thank you readers and listeners, from the bottom of my heart, for taking the time to digest my collective patchwork of poems and personal extracts. Perhaps, one day we shall meet.

And where to begin

My debt of thank yous. My gratitude for those who showed me the greatest compassion when I least deserved it, who endured, who caught glimpses of me, I owe you my life. So, thank you to my husband - your love for me is nothing short of miraculous. Thank you Mary Cook, the best neighbour in the world. Thank you Rev. Eleanor Powell for your wise words and validation. Thank you Rita Thomas - you are my spirit sister. Thank you to Lydia and John Jenkins for saving my life the first time. Thank you Jean Holden for going above and beyond as my Dissertation Tutor. Thank you Julia Carrotte for being a surrogate mum to me all those years ago. Thank you Liz and Tim Lewis for giving me a job when I looked like a scarecrow. Thank you Dr Gemma Timothy for taking the time to look at my notes.

It's Not Just Celery

Thank you Rachel Peach, Kimberly Howe, Emma Tyler, Dr Kelly Young, Cerri Goodfellow, Katie Jones and Sophie Goodridge for your loyal and honest friendship, you are remarkable women. Thank you Chris Noon, for asking the questions I was afraid to - you are kinder and more patient than you know. Thank you Samaritans, for answering the phone to me that particular afternoon. Thank you Abigail and Nathanael Orr at All Create Publishing for effectively being my trusted publishing home, whose passion for unlocking hidden creatives and recognising art in all mediums, not only as a vocation but as a life source, is a gift.

About the Author

Kathryn Gonzales is an author and poet based in Cardiff, Wales where she lives with her husband and miniature long haired dachshund. As a former Peer Mentor, Kathryn has helped, supported and inspired many at "Growing Space," a mental health charity and continues to reach out through her debut book offering "It's Not Just Celery." Diagnosed with Anorexia Nervosa in her teenage years, Kathryn has experienced great struggle and considers both her art-practice & faith as vital elements of her managed recovery & support.

Her poetry has also been displayed in the touring art exhibition "#EmbraceEquity 2023" alongside other female artists work inspired by the stories of biblical women, a response to International Women's Day.

Kathryn is not on any social media platforms. If you would like to get in touch with her, please email Kathryn at kljgauthor@gmail.com.